ON THE HUNT

# PYTHON HUNTING

BY ROXANNE TROUP

EPIC

EPIC, AN IMPRINT OF BELLWETHER MEDIA BY FLUTTERBEE

# EPIC

**EPIC BOOKS** are no ordinary books. They burst with intense action, high-speed heroics, and shadows of the unknown. Are you ready for an Epic adventure?

This edition first published in 2027 by Bellwether Media, Inc.



For information regarding permission, write to Bellwether Media, Inc., Attention: Permissions Department, 3500 American Blvd W, Suite 150, Bloomington, MN 55431.

Library of Congress Cataloging-in-Publication Data

Names: Troup, Roxanne author
Title: Python hunting / by Roxanne Troup.
Description: Minneapolis, Minnesota : Bellwether Media, Inc, 2027. | Series: On the hunt | Includes bibliographical references and index. | Audience: Ages 8-12 | Audience: Grades 4-6 |
Summary: "Engaging images accompany information about python hunting. The combination of high-interest subject matter and light text is intended for students in grades 2 through 7"-- Provided by publisher.
Identifiers: LCCN 2026001590 (print) | LCCN 2026001591 (ebook) | ISBN 9798898800932 (library binding) | ISBN 9798898802172 (ebook)
Subjects: LCSH: Snake hunting--Juvenile literature | Hunting--Juvenile literature
Classification: LCC SK341.S5 T76 2027 (print) | LCC SK341.S5 (ebook)
LC record available at https://lccn.loc.gov/2026001590
LC ebook record available at https://lccn.loc.gov/2026001591

Editor: Ashley Kuehl Designer: Jennifer Bowyer

Printed in the United States of America, North Mankato, MN.

# TABLE OF CONTENTS

# SCOUTING THE DARK

It is a quiet night. Hunters drive slowly down a dirt road. They watch both sides of the road. They shine lights into the grass. They are hunting pythons.

# UNWELCOME GUEST

Pythons are an **invasive species** in the United States. They came from Southeast Asia.

# BURMESE PYTHON RANGE IN THE U.S.

People brought them to the U.S. as pets. Some pets escaped. Others were taken to the Florida **Everglades**.

In the U.S., pythons have few **predators**. They lay up to 100 eggs a year. Their numbers are growing fast.

## BIG GULP

Pythons wind their bodies around the animals they eat. The animals cannot fight. Then the snakes swallow the animals whole.

Pythons eat other animals. Many small animals in the Everglades are nearly gone.

Florida is trying to fix the problem of too many pythons. The state hires hunters to help.

Pythons can be hunted all year. There are no **bag limits**. Hunters do not need a **license**.

## FAVORITE HUNTING SPOT

### EVERGLADES, FLORIDA

- Hosts the Florida Python Challenge, a python-catching contest
- State pays some hunters to remove pythons

# NEEDED GEAR

Pythons are active at night. But so are mosquitoes. Hunters need headlamps and bug spray.

# HUNTING GEAR

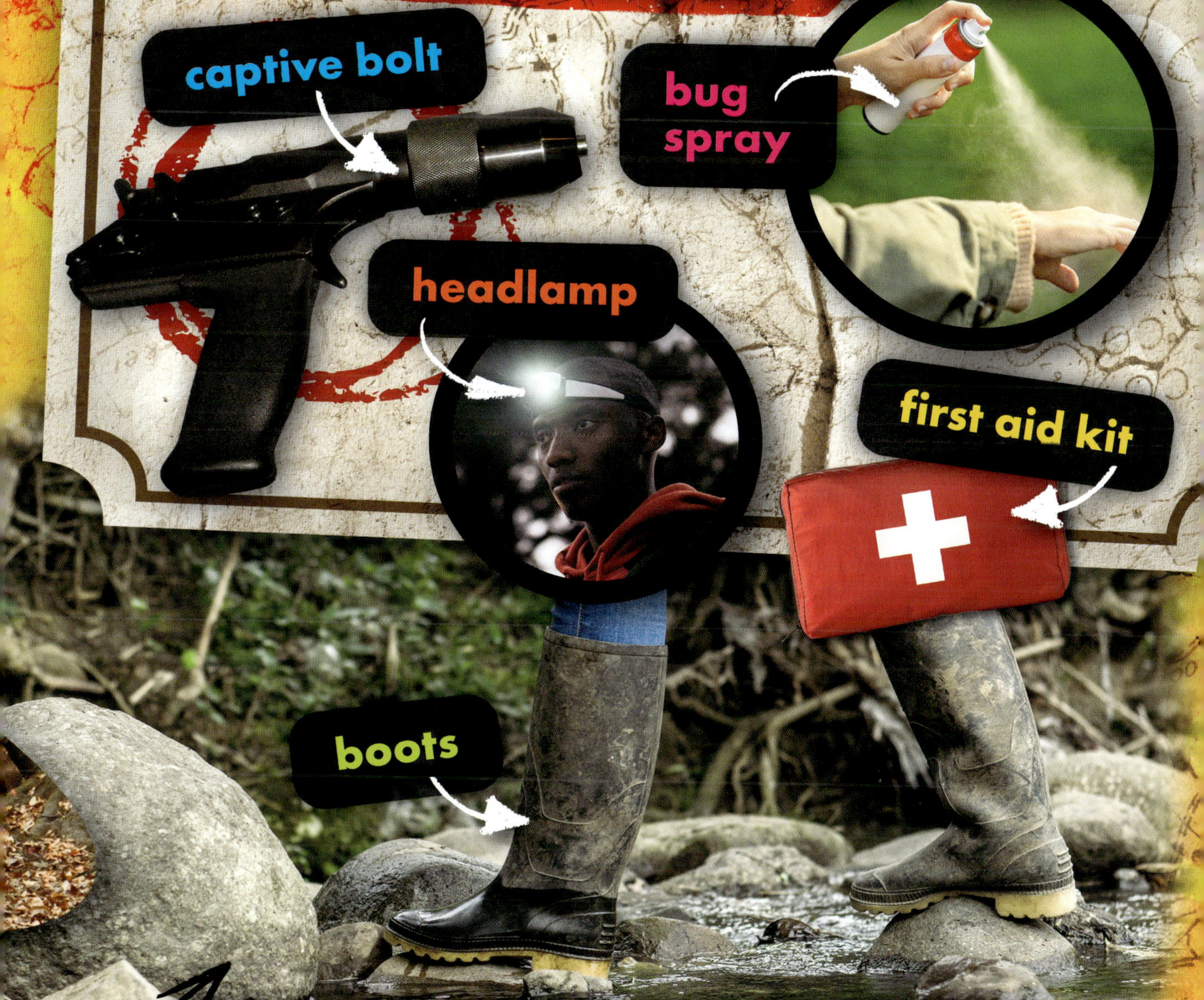


**Wetlands** are covered in **brush** and **poisonous** plants. Long clothing protects skin. A first aid kit can help too.

Pythons are not the only snakes in Florida. Boots protect hunters from snake bites. They also keep feet dry in the wetlands.

Most hunters catch snakes with their hands. They use a **captive bolt** to knock the pythons out. The snakes do not suffer when they die.

## SUPERSIZED SNAKE

Pythons can grow 23 feet (7 meters) long and weigh up to 250 pounds (113 kilograms)! That is one supersized snake!

# A SAFE HUNT

The Everglades are huge! It is easy to get lost. Hunters should stay near roads. They should learn to spot pythons from afar. This will help them stay away from **venomous** snakes.

## NO MORE PETS!

People can no longer keep pythons as pets in Florida. It is also illegal to ship them.

Hunters must decide how to use the animal. The meat is not good for food. But its skin makes nice leather. Hired hunters get cash for their pythons. All of these hunters help fix the Everglades.

snakeskin leather

# GLOSSARY

**bag limits**—the numbers of animals one person is allowed to hunt per day

**brush**—woody plants and tall weeds

**captive bolt**—a tool that hits an animal's brain with a heavy bolt to stun it and keep it from moving

**Everglades**—a wetland in southern Florida

**invasive species**—a species not originally from a region that causes harm to its new region

**license**—a document that give hunters legal permission to harvest a certain type of animal

**poisonous**—causing sickness or death when touched or eaten

**predators**—animals that hunt other animals for food

**venomous**—causing sickness or death when touched or eaten

**wetlands**—areas of land that are covered with low levels of water for most of the year

# TO LEARN MORE

## AT THE LIBRARY

Kaner, Etta. *Beware the Burmese Pythons: And Other Invasive Animal Species.* Toronto, Ontario, Canada: Kids Can Press, 2022.

Messner, Kate. *Tracking Pythons: The Quest to Catch an Invasive Predator and Save an Ecosystem.* Minneapolis, Minn.: Millbrook Press, 2020.

Troup, Roxanne. *Wild Hog Hunting.* Minneapolis, Minn.: Bellwether Media, 2026.

## ON THE WEB

**FACTSURFER**

Factsurfer.com gives you a safe, fun way to find more information.

1. Go to www.factsurfer.com.
2. Enter "python hunting" into the search box and click .
3. Select your book cover to see a list of related content.

# INDEX



The images in this book are reproduced through the courtesy of: Freeograph, front cover, p. 1; Heiko Kiera, front cover, pp. 1, 8; Eric Isselée, front cover, p. 1; Agus Gatam, front cover, p. 1; fivespots, p. 3; CHANDAN KHANNA/ Getty Images, p. 4; Lunatic_67, p. 5; ZUMA Press, Inc./ Alamy Stock Photo, pp. 6, 11; Chokniti Khongchum/ Alamy Stock Photo, p. 7 (profile); wei.hwc, p. 7; Badrudin15, p. 9; Larry Larsen/ Alamy Stock Photo, p. 11 (inset); Phillip W. Kirkland, p. 12; geni/ Wikimedia, p. 13 (captive bolt); Syda Productions, p. 13 (bug spray); Mariusz Szczawinski/ Alamy Stock Photo, p. 13 (headlamp); Shawn Hempel, p. 13 (aid kit); Maurotoro, p. 13; JasonOndreicka, p. 14; Mark_Kostich, p. 14 (inset); Kelly Shannon Kelly/ Alamy Stock Photo, p. 15; Joe Raedle/ Getty Images, p. 16; USGS/ Alamy Stock Photo, p. 17; zef art, p. 18; ROMAN DZIUBALO, p. 19; niuniu, p. 20; Serdar Ba ak/ Alamy Stock Photo, p. 20 (jacket); Madelyn Motsinger, p. 21; Matthijs Kuijpers/ Alamy Stock Photo, p. 23.